101 THINGS I WASN'T TAUGHT IN MY EDUCATION CLASSES

One Teacher's Light-hearted Look at the Unexpected with Practical Warnings and Suggestions

by Jodie Fransen

Incentive Publications
Nashville, Tennessee

Illustrated by Kathleen Bullock
Cover by Geoffrey Brittingham
Edited by Jill Norris
Copy edited by Cary Grayson

ISBN 978-0-86530-504-5

1 2 3 4 5 6 7 8 9 10   11 10 09 08

PRINTED IN THE UNITED STATES OF AMERICA
www.incentivepublications.com

Table of Contents

Introduction

There I was, feeling prepared and eager for my first day of teaching. I had done a solid job of listening to my university professors pass on their knowledge and expertise, and I was ready to go. After a short pause, I turned into the "Faculty Parking" lot, parked, and walked into the place where I had my first "real job." In this school in the fairly affluent district I now called employer, I checked in, put on my name badge, rolled my classroom-on-a-cart into room 312, and thought I owned the world.

Then reality struck. It turns out that all that college tuition and all those knowledgeable professors had prepared me for only a small part of what my future would hold. From my first fateful day in the classroom, I have been utterly amazed at all the things I've experienced as part of teaching that NO ONE told me about ahead of time!

What follows here are 101 of those things. Some are amazing, many are hilarious, and a few are horrifying, but they all add up to the work I love: teaching. Of course no two educators' experiences are exactly the same, and I don't assume all my revelations will match yours, but some will. And no matter what, I do know that there will always be things about teaching that will take you by surprise!

Jodie Fransen

Part 1
Surprises in Dealing with Students

"When I was five everyone told me to be a big boy.
When I was ten they told me I should be more mature.
Now they say it's time to start acting like an adult.
At this rate, I'll be eligible for Social Security before
I graduate from high school."

Chapter 1

Disobedience and the Circle of Life

As a kid, when I did something inappropriate, my parents often took pleasure in telling me to "just wait 'til *you* have kids!" This brings me to the first thing I learned that I wasn't taught in education school.

1 ***All the bad things you did as a student will come back to haunt you as a teacher.*** Whether you were a note passer, a gum chewer, a graffiti artist, chronically tardy, sometimes absent without permission, class clown, or worse, everything you thought of or witnessed (and more!) will once again be a part of your life. In the blink of an eye, it will now be *your* responsibility to notice and resolve every trick and prank, even while it's possible you will secretly take some personal pleasure in the more clever troublemakers. As an aside, I hope the boy named Sam who bounced the frog eyeballs at me in science lab is a teacher now; he deserves whatever he gets! Of course this doesn't apply if you were one of the never-caused-any-problems-in-school types. In that case, you are in for some unhappy surprises.

On the positive side, having background knowledge about misbehavior can often help you be proactive. While there is no way you will anticipate everything your students will try, you will at least have an idea of what might be coming your way. In addition, this chapter includes some of the more interesting forms of disobedience I have witnessed, in an effort to prepare you for what may be coming your way.

There are still plenty of old-fashioned ways for students to cause trouble, even in today's technology-filled schools (more on this later). While I understood there would be discipline issues to deal with, I didn't take into account that . . .

2 *For every rule there are at least a dozen students who spend all their free time figuring out how to creatively break it.* For my first set of examples, I turn to the dress code. In the school where I teach we don't allow baggy pants. One group of boys was so anxious for everyone to see their boxer shorts that they wore them on the *outside* of their jeans. "But we're not wearing baggy pants!" they protested. On a similar note, I had one student who preferred to wear *two* pairs of pants at the same time, one baggy (on the outside) and one not. His response was, "You didn't say *all* my pants couldn't be baggy, just the ones that are supposed to cover my underwear." Fortunately, that student received natural consequences by being unable to walk easily and by tripping up the stairs several different times, usually in front of girls he was trying to impress. (An aside about baggy pants: if you ever start feeling too serious about your job, watch boys in baggy pants try to play basketball or do any type of running. I honestly have seen several students dribble a ball with only one hand because they need the other one to keep them from losing their pants altogether.)

A certain female student of mine also had extreme difficulty adhering to the dress code. In her case, she wore very low cut shirts or tank tops, often with undergarments showing. We thought we were clear each time we informed her about her infractions and made her change clothes, but we didn't anticipate her next move: she came to school wearing a bright red lacy bra under a tiny, skin-tight, white T-shirt that actually belonged to her younger brother. "But I'm covered!" she protested.

Next are the students who wear the inappropriate T-shirts claiming they had no idea there was a double meaning. One such memorable shirt depicted a group of campers sitting around a campfire roasting hotdogs. The caption read, "It's all fun and games until someone loses a wiener." That's subtle! Another common shirt during football season demonstrated the local team's rivalry with the Nebraska Cornhuskers. It read "Huck the Fuskers." Upon being asked to change clothes, the students would usually reply, " . . . but . . . but . . . 'huck' isn't inappropriate!" Sure. And of course there are many other T-shirts depicting bands, stores, restaurants, products, and more that also have no place in school. No one warned me that I would have to be the fashion police in addition to all my other duties!

Next is gum. While there are a wide variety of opinions on whether or not gum should be allowed in schools, it is currently not allowed in mine. The main result of this is students who try anything to keep it in their mouths without getting caught. It follows that teachers at my school spend a ridiculous amount of time trying to catch these gum chewers and break them of their sticky habit. One year we even let the kids "win," and permitted gum as long as it was chewed quietly. The results were more gum in the carpet, more gum under the desks, gum in the drinking fountain, and middle-school entrepreneurs selling gum during lunch recess. The next year we returned to the familiar refrain of "Spit your gum out!" Who knew!

3 ***Even art can be a vehicle for clever disobedience.*** Until I experienced it for myself, I had no idea that motivated students can often put hidden messages or images in an art project with very little chance of being found out. They also put *obvious* messages or images in, probably hoping to be noticed! One of my favorite examples was a collage made out of torn paper that had not-so-subtle male anatomical parts 'hidden' in plain sight. I have also seen pottery with hidden profanity, paintings with disguised drug references, and sculptures of all sorts of unmentionables, all in the name of creative disobedience. Let's hope the students who take their art seriously and the adults who advocate support of the arts don't let this get in their way!

4 ***Some students will use anything available in the classroom to cause trouble.*** I have had students staple themselves, put paperclips in electrical outlets, and tie their neighbor's hands together with masking tape, all in the interest of "seeing what would happen." I also had a particularly resourceful student who would try to get into the classroom before I did so he could erase selected letters off the board and spell new and exciting things. For example, what used to say "Bring a pen to class" might become "B_i_g _ ___ __ __ass." There's probably a life skill there somewhere, but I can't figure out what it might be.

I will conclude this chapter with the one thing no one told me that took me the longest time to get over:

5 ***Not all students are as excited to learn what you're teaching as you are to teach it.*** The reason I decided to become an English teacher was twofold: I love English literature and I love teaching. It probably should have occurred to me that the name "Shakespeare" would cause groans, or playing preposition games wouldn't be thrilling for everyone, but it didn't. This could be because during my entire school experience I was surrounded by students and professors who loved English as much as I do. Of course, over time I have learned how to better relate Shakespeare to everyone and how to make preposition games fun for even the hard-core grammar haters, but that was quite an adjustment for me in the beginning! In any case, do not let this lessen your enthusiasm or love of your work. There are certainly students out there who want to be where you are, and doing what you're doing, and teachers should never forget that they are truly inspirational every day.

"No more school blues . . . "

Chapter 2

Cheating

6 ***A lot of students (from about 5th grade up) think a lot of teachers are stupid, and this will never be as obvious as it is when they are trying to cheat.*** Many students are convinced that they can get away with anything, and cheating is toward the top of that category. While I'm sure students *do* get away with things, I have also learned that the things kids *think* they can get away with vastly outnumber the things they actually pull off.

In my mind, cheating falls into two main categories: old-fashioned and technologically advanced. Let's start with the first one. Many of these methods haven't changed in generations; they still include writing answers on arms and legs, passing answers across the room in a variety of forms, and copying off each other's papers. What I wasn't told was . . .

7 ***For every student motivated to cheat there is an innovative way to try it.*** Some of the newer ones I've experienced include one student taping answers under the desk for the next student who sits there (for a fee, of course), students stealing copies of tests or answer keys, and students from different classes setting times to meet in the restroom to discuss answers. I once had a student write answers on a paper airplane and send it across the room, and I have seen all sorts of hand signals tried, as well as blatant copying. And of course there are those I didn't catch . . . their methods are obviously the best, whatever they are!

In terms of technology, the possibilities for cheating are nearly endless. First, there is the fairly pervasive technique of copying research papers, book reviews, poetry, or other writing from the Internet. The less energetic student will often print things straight from the computer without giving any credit to the original author. Once I even had a student print out an essay and use old-fashioned correction fluid to cover the real author's name! Fortunately technology is also beginning to provide ways to help teachers discover plagiarism fairly easily, but I'm sure some enterprising student will find a way to stay ahead of the advances.

What's more, we now face even more technologically advanced cheating. Today's students often have more computing power in their pockets than any Apollo rocket used to get to the moon. Just a few months ago, my teaching teammate caught a student sending a text message with test answers to a classmate in another room. There are also services that will answer students' questions for free, and it is even possible to surf the Internet for answers during a test using a variety of small devices. Again, schools are catching up to this, but who would have guessed?

"I hacked into the school computer and changed all my grades. Then the school hacked into my computer and deleted all my games!"

Chapter 3

More on Students and Technology

In general, I could never have guessed how technology would virtually take over education. In addition to the cheating tools mentioned above, I quickly learned . . .

8 ***There are almost unlimited positive and negative consequences of students having access to so much technology.*** My first indication that things were changing fast was back in the 90s when a student in my class kept changing the channel on the television with the remote control built into his wristwatch. Fortunately this trend didn't really catch on, but in just the last few years my school has had to make policies about pagers, then cell phones, then text messaging, then hand-held games, then digital camera use, and on it goes. We have also had to bring in guest speakers about Internet dangers and cyber bullying. And finally, as with anything new, students will always push the boundaries. Who would have thought that we would find ourselves disciplining kids for taking inappropriate pictures of each other and sending them to places where anyone could see them? Or posting slanderous things on their online accounts?

Of course these are the extreme cases; much more frequently I find myself dealing with technological silliness like students calling each others' cell phones during class to get their 'friends' in trouble, having arguments about online chats that happened the night before, or sneaking video games into class to fill their time (and, of course, to see if they can get away with it!). I have also witnessed many students trying to change the pictures on desktops or screensavers of school computers to suit their tastes, whether it's with supermodels, rock stars, food, or worse. And for every form of new technological silliness, there is a genius out there trying to counteract it and a middle school student out there trying to overcome the counteraction.

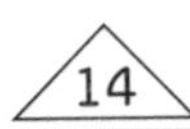

On the plus side, earlier forms of technological silliness like prank phone calls have virtually disappeared with the introduction of caller ID. Also, the quick access to helpful information is mind-boggling. Students and teachers alike can now instantly research anything from a foreign country to a line of poetry to government policy, and on and on. Teaching strategies have been forced to evolve to keep up, and the breadth of students' knowledge about the world (albeit selective) has made exponential leaps. We can also take students on "virtual field trips" almost anywhere without ever leaving the classroom. The lesson here is again to expect the unexpected and to never stop learning, because things really don't stay the same for long.

And finally, . . .

9 ***If you need to learn a new technology, ask a student first!*** I have received many valuable after-school lessons about how to text message, better ways to use my digital camera, how to make my television's digital video recorder work, and how to access all sorts of Internet conveniences. Of course it's not always easy to admit to a 14-year-old that you don't have a clue about something they take for granted, but it can be a great experience for both of you!

Chapter 4

Excuses

There are days at school I refer to as "excuse days." These are the times when projects or papers are due and some students will be pulling out all the stops to explain what happened to theirs. As soon as you think you've heard every excuse, you'll hear a new one. In fact, students don't realize that the time spent making excuses is probably more than the time needed to actually complete the task at hand. Oh well, if everyone completed all their work on time, the creative art of excuse making might be lost forever!

10 ***Some excuses that have been around since the dawn of public education are still being tried today.*** These include "I lost it," "*You* lost it," or "Someone stole it." I won't bother to comment on the black market value of an eighth-grade essay, but suffice it to say that's not the best excuse. Some kids also still use "The dog ate it," "My little brother ate it," or "My mom didn't know what it was and threw it away." As far as I know, these are usually false as well, although I did have one student hand in a paper with actual dog teeth marks in it. His explanation was one word: puppy. At least he turned it in.

11 ***Technology has given students a whole new selection of excuses.*** These include "My printer ran out of ink," "I didn't have any paper for printing," "My computer ate it—one minute it was there and then it wasn't!" or "The power went out and I lost everything." Sometimes students will also try, "I emailed it to you—what do you mean you didn't get it?" or "What do you mean it's not on my storage drive? I swear I saved it!"

12 ***Students with divorced or separated parents also have a varied selection of excuses.*** While there is nothing funny about a student who has to live in two different households, some of them have made the most out of the situation by expanding their excuse repertoire. While I'm sure there is sometimes merit to "It's at my mom's" or "It's at my dad's," I have some trouble with "It's at my step-mom's grandma's office, and I won't see her again until December" or "My mom's old boyfriend has it, and I'm not allowed to call him." For students with a variety of living situations, I suppose this could fall under the making-lemonade-from-lemons category.

13 ***Some excuses are so amazing that all you can do is shrug your shoulders and move on.*** I don't know if this first example is technically an excuse, but it needs to be included for its "huh" factor. A colleague of mine once asked a student who was standing right in front of her to "please sit down." When he didn't respond, she repeated the request more forcefully. He then shot back with "I AM sitting down." Huh?

This brings me to my very favorite excuse of all time, given by an eighth-grade girl who was supposed to be researching lightning for an earth science report. Despite the fact that we had spent several days in the library and the computer lab, her paper contained very little that wasn't common knowledge. She included things like "lightning can be dangerous," "lightning comes in thunderstorms," and "lightning is electric." When I pushed her a little further about her apparent lack of research, she explained: "I don't really know anything about lightning because I hardly ever go outside." Would you have a good response for that one? I didn't.

Chapter 5

The Language Barrier

Part of being a nongrownup is figuring out ways to separate your age group from those you feel are less knowledgeable (or worthy!). The most easily accessible tool for this purpose is language. Kids have always made up their own slang for everything from food to clothes to proclamations of love. The media in all its forms helps with this trend, too, whether with song lyrics, television shows, movies, or the Internet. What I wasn't told is . . .

14 ***There is a good possibility that students might be speaking your language and you have no idea what they're saying.***

Several years ago a student left a note on my desk that said "You're the Bomb." After research (aka asking students), I discovered it was not a death threat, but rather a compliment. "You're so phat," and "That movie was sick," are similar examples of positive comments disguised as negative ones. And don't forget that these expressions change almost by the day; being "phat" next year may well be as bad as being "shifty" was last year.

This doesn't even take into account what technology has done to writing skills. As an English teacher, I am exposed to new ways kids shorten written expressions every year, and I have had to learn all the abbreviations they use not because they're sending me text messages, but because they put them in their essays thinking it's O.K. Terms such as IDK (short for I don't know), LOL (laugh out loud), B/C (because), JK (just kidding), and U (you) are commonplace. I even had a student write "WTF" (what the #@&!) on his paper when he got confused about what to say next. That one required a little extra disciplinary attention!

In the end, the best you can do is try to stay current, don't be shocked when you fall behind, and ask before you assume. After all, this type of "foreign" language is one of the few things kids can claim for their own.

Chapter 6

Other Notable Student Behavior

Even when I thought I was completely prepared for every imaginable classroom contingency, no one ever told me that . . .

15 ***There will always be at least one kid who knows more than you do.*** No matter the topic, your class will have an expert. This doesn't even account for the kids who just think they're experts. From experience, I can confidently tell you . . .

16 ***Don't be afraid to admit you don't know something.*** It's much better than attempting to make something up and being proven wrong by a ten-year-old. On the other side, don't get into a long-winded argument with a student who thinks he's right even if you know you are. Make a comment like "I'll look into it," then bring in your proof and restate your case when there isn't an audience for your little genius to impress.

I have to admit I was partially taught this next one:

17 ***Students ask really stupid questions.*** I have also learned that this is the case for people in all walks of life, and even teachers ask more than a few stupid questions once in a while. What I wasn't prepared for was the extent of the problem in class and my own confusion over what an appropriate response should be. Here is a sampling of a few stupid questions I have encountered repeatedly:

"Do we have to put our names on our papers?"
"Did we do anything while I was absent?"
"Do we have to do this?"
"Do I need anything for this class?"
And my personal favorite, "Are we doing anything today?"

There is also the time-honored, "Is this going to be on the test?" which is not always as stupid as teachers think it is.

There is also an entire category of stupid questions I call "What if's." A favorite pastime of students everywhere seems to be thinking up the most unusual scenario they can and asking the teacher about it. These might include questions like, "What if I get chased by a rabid dog and drop my homework in the gutter?" "What if a terrorist steals my essay?" "What if I get sick the day I'm supposed to give my presentation?" and "What if my baby brother spits up on my project?"

I have also discovered that sometimes it really doesn't matter how hard the teacher tries to counteract these types of questions. For example, I have posted the current date on the wall of my classroom every day for 20 years, yet every day at least one student blurts out, "What day is it?"

Of course one challenge here is that most teachers are taught to encourage questions, and many questions are helpful for the bridge to knowledge they provide. So what do you say to a really stupid question? One option is to unleash your inner comedian. For example, my favorite response to "Did we do anything while I was absent?" is "No, we just stared at your empty desk for 45 minutes." In the cases of what-if's, I recommend a redirection to the effect of, "What if your brother *doesn't* spit up on your work?" or "What if aliens beam your work into a black hole?" followed by, "We can only deal with what we know and not worry about what-if's." Sometimes this response actually works.

Unfortunately not everyone thinks I'm as funny as I do, so I have come to terms with . . .

18 ***Sometimes no response is the best response.*** On many occasions, the students themselves will call each other on stupid questions, or the questioner will realize the error of his or her ways. On other occasions, it's best just to withhold the sarcasm you are tempted to use and get to the root of the problem. Is the student really confused? Do they just want attention? Is their brain in another part of the world? Is asking stupid questions part of their plot to take over the classroom? You have to decide. In any case as a reminder to myself that I am not alone, I have a poster on my classroom wall that summarizes the conflict between encouraging kids and calling them on their lack of knowledge. It shows a teacher in the form of a goose surrounded by little gosling students. She is addressing one with something like, 'While there is no such thing as a stupid question, if there were such a thing, that certainly would have been it.' In its own politically correct way, that has summarized my thoughts on many occasions.

The final two things in this category that surprised me when I began teaching relate primarily to adolescents, although there are probably examples of these things happening with other students as well. First is . . .

19 ***Kids have a strange physical need to throw things in class.*** While I have no specific scientific data to back this up, I have plenty of anecdotal and experiential evidence. There are always students who throw things no matter what lengths you go to in trying to alleviate the problem. This includes the kid who, when asked to borrow a pencil, tosses it from one side of the room to the other. This also includes the kid who just has to "make a basket" with his wad of paper by throwing it toward the trash can. Other kids have been known to toss notes, textbooks, or even scissors (again this one needs disciplinary action!). This doesn't include the kids who throw things as a form of revenge or who figure out ways to "shoot" things using rubber bands, empty pen cylinders, or other available tools. I have no explanation for this behavior, but I do recommend trying to channel it in some way if you can because it *will* happen.

The next lesson I learned the hard way was . . .

20 ***If a student asks you to borrow something, always ask why.*** One time a student asked to borrow note cards; silly me, I thought they were to take notes for research. Then he started to build a tower out of them (and soon asked for tape to finish the project!). I have had kids ask for markers only to turn them into swords, kids ask for paper clips only to make them into miniature sculptures, and kids ask for adhesive bandages only to use five of them to repair a tear in their notebook. While these students could probably be praised for "thinking outside the box," you should nonetheless be prepared if you don't want all of your supplies to disappear for no good reason.

Then there is the regrettable fact that . . .

21 ***Students can be really mean to each other.*** I suppose it boils down to low self-esteem or power struggles, but no one warned me how well students can figuratively crush each other, or of the fallout that can result. This usually takes two forms: obvious and subtle. The first category includes students who have no reservations about hurling insults related to looks, clothes, hair, intelligence, and more. The second includes passing gossipy notes, spreading rumors, hiding notebooks, and a myriad of other possibilities. Both boys and girls are capable of astounding meanness in many forms, and teachers are wise to expect it so that it can be handled sooner rather than later.

And finally, we get to hair.

22 ***Never underestimate the importance of hair to a middle-school student.*** Whether it's long, short, blue, striped, shaved, braided, corn-rowed, or anything in between, more students will be thinking about their hair than their classwork at any given time during the day. And that's if all is well, follicle-y speaking; if a student has had a recent haircut tragedy, an unfortunate dye job, or even a bad hair day, the amount of things he or she can be expected to accomplish during the day just took a dive.

In my school, the sink and mirror part of the student restrooms are visible from the hallway. I never pass one of these without seeing at least one student working on hair. This is true for boys as well as girls, and the plethora of hair products available today has only added to this issue. Sometimes this aspect of student appearance even requires assistance; yes, it really can take two students to make one student's hair look just the way it's supposed to. One way teachers can take advantage of this situation is quite simple: compliment students about their hair whenever it's appropriate. You might be amazed at what it means to them!

And finally, if you still have reason to doubt the importance of hair, see what happens when you change yours. I guarantee that any change will be noticed and will probably give rise to comments. These include, "Did you change your hair?" "What did you do to your hair?" and (if you're lucky) "I like your hair." One of my favorites was when I answered yes to "Did you cut your hair?" and the follow-up comment was, "I liked it better before." Clearly teaching is no job for those who lack self-confidence!

"If I do my homework, I'll get good grades.
If I get good grades, I'll go to college.
If I go to college, I'll graduate and get a job.
If I get a job, I might get fired.
If I get fired, I might lose everything.
That's why I didn't do my homework."

Part 2
Surprises in Dealing with Grownups

"I'm in over my head!"

Chapter 7

Teachers and Technology

Most things related to teaching change in some way as each year passes. New methodologies will be developed, new textbooks will be written, and motivational techniques will advance with the times. Nowhere is this change more noticeable, however, than in the area of technology. Keep in mind that I graduated from education school when VCRs were new (and huge!), we still used "typing paper," and only science fiction characters had tiny portable phones. No one could possibly have prepared me for all that was to come, how rapidly it would advance, or the fact that I would be surprised by technology almost every day.

23 ***Technology (or the lack of it) controls teachers' lives in unexpected ways.*** First of all, in my classroom, the temperature is regulated by a computer at the education center some ten miles away. It follows that my comfort level (and that of my students) is completely dependent on computer data and not on real people with real personal thermostats! No one told me that needing a coat in the room in August or sweating like crazy in January were actual possibilities, but they happen. I learned fairly quickly that the only one capable of remedying these issues is a person named Trudy*—who sits at a desk at the main education center and requires a phone call to adjust anything. Of course teachers can't call; she will listen to only one person from each school who fields the complaints, and in our building it's the head secretary. After this two-step process, the adjustment often takes hours, and seeing the results takes even longer. My hard-earned lesson here is to dress in layers (and be nice to the secretary—more on this later). Students, however, are normally more concerned with making fashion statements than being comfortable, and who can blame them?

**not her real name, to protect her (and me!)*

When they get that new sweater they've been saving up for, they want to wear it to school and show it off. How would they know that the classroom might be 80 degrees that day? At the same time, when short-skirt and tank-top season arrives, what girl wants to cover up her ensemble with a sweatshirt? The fallout of these unpredictable weather moments can range from shivering students to smelly, sweaty students to massively overheated students with nearly comatose stares.

At this point I do have to give a salute to the many teachers whose schools have poor or no air conditioning and/or heat. The first middle school I taught in had no air conditioning and terrible ventilation, and we would have given most anything to be freezing in August. Instead we dealt with sweaty (and usually stinky) students for several months a year and rode around in our air-conditioned cars over lunch to reduce our body temperatures. It's probably good that we didn't know about the teachers shivering in the air-conditioned cold just a few miles away!

24 ***Access to technology in the classroom (or the lack of it) can mean everything.*** Obviously, each school is different and has a variety of tools at its disposal. The more modern schools in my district have wireless Internet, multiple printers (black & white and color), phones and TV's in every room, computer projectors, DVD players, "smart boards," well-equipped computer labs, and a budget to keep everything current. The older buildings have phones to share, overloaded computer systems, and old-fashioned chalk boards complete with the white dust. In any case, I have found that many schools share the same issues, and that . . .

25 ***Most schools have these six technology problems in common:***

- By the time you get a new device of any sort, a better one will already exist (and some students will have one of whatever it is).
- When something can go wrong, it will. Even one button on a remote control can mess up an entire day!

- As soon as you learn to use a given technology, something better will be invented and you'll need to learn how to use that one.

- There is rarely enough money to buy the latest equipment. In the event that there is, there won't be enough money to maintain it.

- There are never enough school technology experts to go around because they are all getting rich in the private sector.

- The district's technology department is also overwhelmed and understaffed as they attempt to deal with the above issues on a large scale.

There is no doubt that technology will march forward. My hope is that schools everywhere will be able to keep up and teachers everywhere will learn to deal with more technological surprises every year.

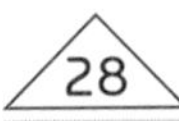

Chapter 8

The Field Trip

In an effort to get students "out in the real world," many teachers consider planning and taking a field trip. Most people remember taking field trips as a student, and the trips usually involved getting in a small group, climbing on the bus, and going somewhere educational and/or entertaining. In most cases there would be a tour, a presentation, or a show to be experienced, then everyone would return to school none the worse for wear.

What no one told me was what goes on behind the scenes of field trip planning and execution. In a nutshell, field trips are an incredible amount of work for the planners! Here are some details I didn't expect.

26 ***Field trip challenges begin with finding a suitable date on the school calendar***. Things such as weather, bus availability, and schedule conflicts must be considered, and if you're lucky you'll happen upon one or two good possibilities for your adventure. Chances are also good that after you have scheduled your trip someone will have a problem with it. The best you can hope for is to avoid negatively impacting as many people as possible.

Then you have to realize that . . .

27 ***Field trip itineraries are serious business; determining what will be going on and how to keep everyone suitably occupied for the allotted time is a monumental task.*** There is a fine line between giving students too much unstructured time and running them ragged. For example, the seventh graders in my school always take a trip to the local zoo. The goals of the trip include learning about the classifications of creatures, studying the adaptations of various animals to their habitats, and increasing environmental awareness. The question becomes how to best accomplish those goals. Should the students be given a huge packet to fill out as they walk around? Or is a one-sheet summary adequate? Or should they just be trusted to walk around and learn as they go without having to write at all? Of course there will be pros and cons for each choice, but who knew there would be so many choices!

28 ***You may need a class in accounting to handle the field trip money.*** How much does the trip cost? How will you get there? How much are the buses? Who will pay? What about kids that can't afford to pay? Will you need to collect money from the students? In short, get organized now! You obviously can't leave money lying around in any form, and it's imperative to know who has paid and who hasn't; so get your spreadsheet ready ahead of time. Kids will also bring in all forms of currency: checks, cash, coins, and even an occasional IOU. Be prepared.

Next, be aware that . . .

29 ***You are legally responsible for field trip paperwork.*** In a perfect teaching world, everyone would bring permission slips and money in on time with the proper signature. Then there's reality. Reality in this case includes making last-minute calls, figuring out who forged their parents' names (easily spotted, though don't try to tell a teenager that), making last-minute duplicate copies, and digging wadded-up forms out of lockers or backpacks.

If all goes well, everyone will be ready to go. If not, there is another surprise . . .

30 ***You have to figure out what to do with kids who aren't going with you.*** Normally the alternatives are finding another teacher or staff member to supervise them or encouraging them to stay home. If they are being supervised at school, it is usually your responsibility to keep them busy. Sometimes this means inventing a six-hour activity for one student, which most people (including me) will tell you is not the best use of your time.

Then, of course . . .

31 ***You will need to be ready for all sorts of "Field Trip What-Ifs."*** In this case, the what-ifs often come true. What if someone gets sick? What if someone can't be found? What if someone forgets to bring lunch? What if the buses are late? What if the museum isn't ready when you get there? What if there's an emergency? What if the weather doesn't cooperate? All these contingencies need to be dealt with long before departure, because some of them will probably happen each time you venture out.

Have you thought about the fact that . . .

32 ***Finding field trip supervisors can be a challenge.*** How many teachers will be able to go? Will there be additional supervisors at the final destination? Should parents be invited? What does the student-to-adult ratio need to be? The answers to each of these questions bring on more questions. If you are taking parents, discretion is very important! For every wonderful and helpful parent chaperone, there is the one who doesn't supervise well, behaves worse than the kids, or does something inappropriate like spend all his time in the museum gift shop or buy everyone in her group candy. I've also had parents who want to negotiate; for example, "I'll come but I won't ride the bus," or "I'll come if I can bring my four other children," or "I'll come but only if I get to choose which students I'm supervising." Without being too rude, I generally explain to these parents that I have many more things to be concerned about than their chaperone happiness level, and then I look for more willing (and flexible) volunteers.

33 ***Students who have special needs in school have even more special needs outside of school.*** For every field trip I've been on, there have been medicines to dispense, allergies to be aware of, physical limitations to overcome, and a variety of other needs to meet. Most of these needs are known ahead of time, but occasionally you will run into some surprises. For example, once I toured our local museum with a girl who informed me that she was terrified of escalators. The result was that we had to go several minutes out of our way to find an elevator or stairs every time we wanted to see a different exhibit. I've also held students' shaky hands in the darkness of a planetarium show, learned how to use an epi-pen®, helped a student give himself an insulin shot, and dispensed an endless variety of pills and inhalers, all while supervising dozens of other kids in a new (and often strange) environment.

34 ***Even some of your best students will misbehave on field trips.*** Because field trips by nature are usually more unstructured than the classroom environment, students tend to try to be more unstructured as well. Even under the best supervision, the kids who are really looking for trouble can usually find it. In particular I recommend you be especially alert in places that are dark or loud, or in the presence of valuable artifacts or wild animals. The best you can do is set the ground rules, plan for contingencies, and expect the unexpected!

35 ***No matter how well you plan your field trip, something unexpected (and probably not good) will happen.*** Here are a few of my more notable field trip adventures:

- Two girls getting into a fist fight over a boy during our end-of-the-year celebration field trip
- Motion sickness (students AND parents) No more to say there.
- One of my parent chaperones needing to be reined in when he swore like a sailor every few minutes, often at passing vehicles
- A middle-school student 'bumming a cigarette' off a college student while touring our local university's planetarium
- Students thrilled over uncovering a rattlesnake nest full of babies on a geology field trip to the mountains
- Blowing snow in May that occurred after we were all at the national park to see the dinosaur fossils Since we were unable to get off the bus, the helpful docents got on and attempted to talk us through what the fossils *looked* like (not especially captivating, even though we tried to pretend it was).

This doesn't even cover the "outdoor education" week.

36 ***You may actually have to stay overnight with your students.*** No one told me I'd be camping out with sixth graders for four consecutive nights. If you knew my personality and need for control, you would know that this information may have been enough to cause me to turn down my first job offer. In fact it wasn't as bad as I thought it would be, but it was certainly a departure from the classroom in many ways. To help your imagination, take all the adventures above and add the unpredictability of nature; you get the idea! Of course I know that there are teachers out there who love outdoor education and who thrive in the unstructured realm of nature, but I'm not one of them. A little heads-up would have been nice!

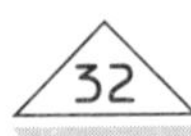

Chapter 9

Embarrassing Moments

Everyone has embarrassing moments. What I was never told was that . . .

37 ***Many embarrassing moments will happen in front of a whole room of students.*** In such cases, it can take a long time to recover one's dignity or, in some cases, classroom control! Of course each experience is unique, but there are a few things I've learned to expect over the years, even though no one warned me ahead of time.

38 ***There will be slips of the tongue.*** For example, every year a student in life science will be reading aloud and mispronounce "organism." Expect it. There are also accidental (and nonaccidental but not meant to be heard) name mess-ups, profanity, or misused words. A wonderful story comes from a friend of mine who was teaching sixth grade. The students had completed projects by applying many different parts of "Bloom's Taxonomy" to a book they had just read. The final product involved stapling the components into spheres, and then hanging them on strings from the ceiling of the classroom. My colleague was so impressed with their work when she first saw the results that she announced, "Your balls look great hanging from the ceiling!" It was a long recovery from that one.

39 ***Words with alternate meanings may become an important part of life.*** For example, when I was in school a "thong" was a shoe. In today's world, telling a student you like her thongs may result in a police summons. As an English teacher I also run into archaic language on a regular basis. Reading Dickens introduces alternative meanings of words such as 'gay' and 'intercourse'; try getting past those and into the thematic meaning of the story. While I am generally jaded and no longer embarrassed by the giggles that sometimes occur, my aging Victorian Literature professor never mentioned this teaching obstacle!

40 ***Beware of mass media; even when you're careful, any form of it can cause embarrassing moments.*** No one told me that having students bring in magazines to be cut up for collages would be an exercise in bravery on my part. Even some of the most wholesome of magazines have ads for lingerie, birth control, or Viagra®; dangerous dealings for early adolescents! The same is true for newspapers. As our societal filter seems to loosen, the contents of mainstream media seem to keep pace. I used to do a "newspaper scavenger hunt" as part of my curriculum, having students look for a variety of information in our local daily paper. Then I found myself repeatedly telling students to look past the "Singles Seeking . . ." ads, the autopsy photos, and the details of torrid affairs and resulting crimes. I stopped fighting it, and we now have other ways of exploring our local paper. Who knew?

And of course this was print media; the potential for embarrassment on the Internet is endless! One missed letter in a URL and your day can be ruined, especially if you happen to be projecting your screen for all to see.

41 ***A personally embarrassing moment for a teacher may become legendary to students.*** Stories of teachers with unzipped flies, spinach in the teeth, bad hair days, visible undergarments, lunch-stained clothes, or intestinal distress may be passed down for generations. Things one person could normally get over pretty quickly can take on a life of their own in a school. As I have learned this lesson, I have adapted. One day a few years ago I was taken over by food poisoning during the school day. Fortunately it was the end of class just before lunch, and the students were all making their way into the hall; but things were happening fast, internally speaking. My options were to run through that hall full of students and attempt to make it to the bathroom, or throw up in my classroom trashcan after everyone left. After briefly considering which option would have fewer witnesses, I chose the second one. Although I had to apologize profusely to the custodian, no students ever found out, and to me that was definitely worth the trade!

And now for some important advice related to embarrassing moments. If you remember one thing from this entire book, it should be . . .

42 ***ALWAYS preview every video, CD, DVD, article, song, story, etc., before you use it in the classroom. Entirely! Every time!*** The only thing worse than a somewhat expected embarrassing moment is an unexpected one. And just because a video comes from a library doesn't mean anything in terms of appropriateness. Just ask the World Languages teacher at my school who decided at the last minute to show a seemingly innocuous video about South American culture and found herself and her class watching graphic animal sacrifices. Teachers have gotten themselves in real trouble by not previewing their materials. Sometimes it's funny, but sometimes it goes beyond amusing and into dangerous territory. No one told me this, but I'm telling you now. Believe me!

"It's important to stay at least one step ahead of the students."

Chapter 10

Staff Hierarchy and Bad Behavior

One of the things I hated when I was in school was the whole popular/not popular thing. There were cliques, labels, and unspoken rules about who was allowed where. And in my naíve world, I thought all that would change when I was on the other side of the teacher's desk. Wrong! So get ready . . .

43 ***Every school has a staff hierarchy, and you'd be smart to learn yours as soon as possible.*** Schools are a complicated network of politics, relationships, expectations, and sometimes drama. Figuring out who is at the top of the proverbial heap may be the only thing standing between you and a disaster at some future time.

Make sure early on that you . . .

44 ***Get to know your secretaries!*** In my school, the people with the most power are the secretaries. They are a cohesive group of highly capable ladies who can make or ruin your entire day (or even year). They also hold grudges. While they are in no way any teacher's *official* "boss," they are responsible for making things run smoothly behind the scenes. If you want to order anything, get reimbursed for anything, schedule anything, get a key for anything, or even (as mentioned earlier) work to change the temperature in the classroom, they are the ones to ask.

The secretary of the very first school I worked in was an attractive, extremely competent, and *very* scary woman. She insisted on "please" and "thank you" at all times, and would let you know if you were doing anything remotely impolite. I will never forget bounding happily into her office the week I was hired, flashing my best big smile, and saying, "Hi! I'm Jodie and I'm here to get my keys!" Her response, with no sign of humor whatsoever, was, "I think you mean, 'May I please have my keys?'" Ouch. I didn't speak directly to her for three months after that, but I did learn a good lesson about power. She had it, I didn't, and she let me know exactly where I stood!

The next power brokers are the custodians, leading me to advise you that you should . . .

45 ***Never underestimate the importance of people who clean up after you and repair things for you.*** No matter what kind of job you do of cleaning your own space, there will be a time when you need the services of a custodian. Chances are it will probably be immediately after a huge mess you don't want to deal with (including bodily fluids) or after you've broken something. This part of your school staff may do most of their work behind the scenes, but they still have lots of power!

The third powerful group in my school is referred to as the "workroom ladies." These are the people who make copies, transparencies, enlargements, and booklets. They also perform the jobs no one wants, like cutting things into little pieces and making sure no one runs out of office supplies. They deserve your respect, too, if only for the simple fact that they are doing the jobs no one else wants!

Next in the hierarchy is usually the administration. What I didn't know was that they, too, are almost entirely dependent on secretaries, custodians, and the workroom ladies! If you're lucky, you will have a caring and competent administrator to lead you and your school. If you're not, you have two options: hang in there, do your best work, and try to outlast him or her; or find work somewhere else. Trying to fundamentally change your administrator is about like trying to fundamentally change your spouse after 20 years of marriage; subtle tweaking might be possible, but wholesale change is not!

I need to mention here that although every school has a hierarchy, it doesn't necessarily mean that the people at the top mistreat the people at the bottom. If your school climate is positive, it's very possible for everyone to feel important and valued. And to do your part, as you climb the invisible ladder, make sure everyone below you feels important and valued, too!

That said, though, the next thing no one told me that I picked up on rather quickly was . . .

46 ***It is a very good idea to be extra nice to those with power.*** Honestly, when I started teaching I paid very little attention to how or when my room got cleaned, how my mail got in my mailbox, who took my field trip money to the bank, who decided what went in the newsletter, or who would be around to make last-minute copies if I had a crisis. Big mistake. I have since learned that every teacher needs help in many ways, and the power of a thank-you note, a kind word, a plate of cookies, or a holiday card can be amazing.

When it comes to the teachers themselves, the next thing I wasn't told was . . .

47 ***Even among professionals, there are cliques, labels, and unspoken rules.*** Some of these are perceived and some are actual, and I should say that my building is full of people working hard to bridge every possible divide. But the groups are still there! It's also important to know that many teachers belong to more than one group, and some people are very happy with their circumstances. Some are not, though, and I discovered that I had a lot to learn about how a group of teachers operates.

A few of the notable groups at my school are the rule sticklers, the wild bunch, the hangers-on-until-retirement, the rookies, the nature lovers, and the loners (technically not a "group," but you get the point). These groups may bond at faculty meetings, at parties, at protests, at "new teacher orientation," on bike rides, or not at all. There are also the teachers who have the reputation of always having the ear of the administrators, either because they're respected, persistent, or just plain loud. Some groups look down their noses at others, while some groups pay little attention to what else is going on. In this complicated microcosm of society we call school, "teacher" only begins to describe the people who educate the children.

When I was a student I couldn't imagine any of my own teachers doing anything other than teaching, so I had no idea that . . .

48 ***Teachers sometimes have really bad (aka law-breaking) behavior.*** And I'm not talking about calling in "sick" to play golf; I'm talking felony convictions. Of course all teachers are closely screened before being hired, but it is not unheard of for a few less scrupulous types to pass initial inspection. In my very well-respected and high-performing district alone there have been affairs, restraining orders (between teachers!), embezzlement, secret 'meetings' in closets, and computer hacking. And those are just the things I know about! If you watch television or read the paper you know that these types of shenanigans go on everywhere. I guess it should have occurred to me that there are not-so-honorable people in every profession, and once I started paying closer attention I realized that it's always the exceptions that make the news; the vast majority of teachers are doing their jobs well and not getting any attention for it. Nonetheless, I never imagined that today's coworker might be tomorrow's inmate.

On a much lighter note, there is the general teacher partying. In my case, when I started teaching I had no kids, no spouse, and not so much as a goldfish to tie me down. Every Friday found me at the local hangout, often with other teachers. What I should have known but didn't was . . .

49 ***If you do something stupid in public, you will hear about it later.*** Of course the amount of damage to your reputation will depend on a number of factors, including how small your town is and what kind of mischief you've been up to. One friend of mine (who shall remain unnamed) made some bad choices ten years ago and is still known around town as "the teacher who danced on the table." When in doubt, have your rowdier staff gatherings in an adjacent county if at all possible!

And finally, just know . . .

50 ***There will be school scandals.*** Maybe it's the fact that schools are the center of many communities, but whenever something unusual happens it is capable of becoming a scandal. Events such as colleagues becoming roommates, teachers getting speeding tickets, or unexpected leaves of absence can quickly become the talk of the town. Nonevents can also give rise to rumors and subsequent scandals, so be prepared!

The lesson from all of this? Teachers are human. Although expected to be superhuman on many occasions, they are not. Once again, it is important to prepare for the worst, expect the best, and enjoy the ride. Just be sure to see who's watching before you enjoy it too much.

Chapter 11

Parents

The world of teaching can often seem isolated. It is important to remember, however, that outside of school every student has a parent or guardian (or two). Most parents are supportive, helpful, and have only their child's best interest in mind. Then there are the other ones. Inevitably, you can . . .

51 ***Show me a student with "issues," and I'll show you a matching parent!*** Many parents think that they are experts about education because they went to school. Those who feel this way may also feel compelled to question you, harass you, or just take up a lot of your time. Rather than generalize further, I will share a few examples.

One of my favorites involved a student who was caught cheating. Prior to arriving to Life Science class, he had copied most of the periodic table of the elements onto his calf. He then accessed this information during a test by crossing his legs and hiking up his jeans. He was, of course, caught by the teacher, who called his mother to explain the situation and discuss options. After some thought, the mother asked, "Did he have the entire periodic table on his leg?" The teacher wasn't sure what was coming next, but answered truthfully, "No, just most of it." The mother's next question: "Can he get partial credit for the answers he *didn't* have on his leg?" Let's just say that took a while to sort out.

My next example comes from a parent who decided to call me at 7:30 in the morning on the first day back from a two-week winter break. She ranted and raved for close to 15 minutes about a book her daughter had brought home to read during her time away from school. How could I assign such a thing? What kind of teacher was I? How dare I? When she slowed down enough for me to get a word in, I simply asked, "Did you read the book?" and she said, "Well, no. But I read the cover and I didn't like it."

Yet another example involves divorced parents who disagreed about something that seemed pretty basic to me: the name of their child. The child's legal name was something like Sara Elizabeth Becker. From the first day of school we called her (not surprisingly!) Sara Becker. After her dad moved out and a custody battle ensued, her mom insisted on calling Sara by a name Mom preferred (in this case Sara's middle name and Mom's maiden name). Of course she didn't bother to pass this information on to any of Sara's teachers.

The best part was the first time postdivorce when she called me and wanted to check on the progress of her daughter Elizabeth Jones. She asked specific questions about an assignment we were working on, so I knew her daughter had to be one of my students, yet I had no idea who she was. I was certain by that time that I was either losing my mind or on hidden camera somewhere. How could I have had a student in my class for months and have no idea who she was?

While these thoughts were churning through my mind, Ms. Jones kept talking and asking questions. Panic began to take over. How would I discuss someone's progress if I didn't have a clue who was being discussed? Finally I asked Ms. Jones to hold while I got some information from my computer. During that time, I actually ran from room to room asking my teammates who the heck Elizabeth Jones was. The first three didn't know, but our math teacher had a brainstorm: he had heard Sara's brother refer to her as Elizabeth; could that be the same person?

Eureka! I returned to the phone and tried to cover by casually asking, "When did you start calling her Elizabeth?" I knew I had the right person then, because the mom launched into a diatribe about how she had always wanted to name 'the baby' Elizabeth, but her obnoxious husband named her Sara instead, and how she would never use the name Becker again, and on and on . . . .
So I solved the mystery of Elizabeth Jones but I still have no clue about the mysterious behavior of some parents!*

**true story, false names*

Part 3
Still More Surprises

"I'm ready for whatever comes my way."

"Aren't there enough problems in the world, anyway?"

Chapter 12

Holidays

There are so many ways that students' personal lives affect their school lives that it would be foolish to try to count them. There is one area that continually surprises me, however, and that is the importance of holidays. While I have always known that holidays are a big deal to kids, what I was never told was how that fact of life wreaks havoc on the events of the classroom. No matter the intended purpose of the celebration, I learned very quickly . . .

52 ***Every holiday takes on a life of its own in a school setting.*** The 'fun' starts with the first major holiday of the school year: Halloween. For most kids, Halloween means the two Cs, costumes and candy. In the classroom, though, I quickly learned that it goes even further, beginning with the fact that . . .

53 ***Halloween costumes at school present numerous challenges.*** First there is the ever-present argument about whether kids should wear their costumes to school, bring them and change into them, or skip the concept altogether. If students do have to change clothes, that comes with its own set of issues, including where and when. Next, there are costume guidelines. Will kids be allowed to dress like bloody vampires or axe murderers or devils? Can boys dress like girls? Can girls dress like French maids? And when should we have the party? If it's at the beginning of the day, everyone will feel sick for hours, and very little learning will take place. If it's at the end of the day, no one will be able to think of or focus on anything else and, again, very little learning will take place! The questions never end. And the kid dressed benignly like a box of cereal or a bumblebee has the added problem of actually fitting in his desk. Next there's the accessory issue. Can the "heiress" bring her poodle? Can the "pirate" bring his sword? And finally there's hair and makeup. Many a middle-school bathroom has been turned into what looks like a crime scene by costumed students seeking to refresh their blue hairspray, white face paint, or fake blood.

54 ***Halloween candy will drive teachers crazy.*** From about the first of September on, when the "fun size" candy appears in the stores, kids will be bringing it to school. This means an increase in trash, an increase in kids begging each other for more candy, an increase in

messes, and an increase in kids on candy highs, followed by an increase in kids wanting naps. This excitement ramps up in mid-October and doesn't end until about the tenth of November when most kids have exhausted their supplies. And remember we're not just talking candy bars; there are sour things, marshmallow things, and little tubes of colored sugar which, in my opinion, shouldn't even be allowed to call themselves candy at all!

Here are a few other random Halloween issues I never saw coming:

55 ***Some families keep their kids home on Halloween for a variety of reasons.*** For example, in my community one Wiccan family kept the kids home to celebrate in private, while a different family kept the kids home because they felt it was satanic to acknowledge Halloween at all. I know of yet other families who have kept their kids home because of phobias, allergies, and fear of inappropriate costumes. Almost anything's possible! Maybe next year I should channel this energy by staying home and claiming candy-phobia.

56 ***Teachers need costumes, too.*** Every year you will probably be pressured to wear something fabulous, usually including a theme or at least something clever, current, and appropriate. I have seen teachers dressed as tacos, current presidents, witches, prom queens, farmers, dogs, and everything in between. Trust me when I say the 30 minutes spent supervising lunchtime dressed as a taco can't go fast enough.

57 ***Some kids will try to get out of going to class because they're "afraid."*** They may claim to be scared of another's costume, whether it's vampires, skeletons, or even clowns. They may claim to be scared of the very *idea* of witches and vampires. They may claim to be scared that they'll run out of candy. Or they may actually be scared of seeing their teacher dressed like a taco!

58 ***In my town, every interest group has something to say about Halloween.*** For example, the LGBT* community advocates Halloween cross-dressing as a form of freedom for questioning teens. A right-wing religious group wants it banned from schools altogether. Animal rights activists, liberals, conservatives, vegetarians, men, women, you name it; everyone has an opinion about Halloween in schools, and most people don't hesitate to share it either with teachers, administrators, or the local newspaper.

**lesbian, gay, bisexual, and transgendered*

59 ***November 1st will always be a total loss at school, too.*** This is due to a variety of factors, including sleep deprivation or sugar headaches. No one in teacher school told me any of this! As a final comment on this specific holiday, I do have a recommendation for lawmakers across America: let's permanently move Halloween to the last Saturday in October. This would essentially buy teachers and students everywhere at least one extra day of learning, if not two or three! Write your congressmen and congresswomen!

The next big holiday on the calendar is Thanksgiving. Fortunately, this has managed to avoid commercialization and is thus widely ignored in schools everywhere. Most elementary schools manage a commemoration or history lesson, but that's about it. The other good news here is that Thanksgiving provides a wide variety of options for crafts, writing assignments, projects, and exercises in gratitude. Who can forget making turkeys out of their handprints? Enjoy this one while it lasts, because December is just around the corner, and believe me, . . .

60 ***After Christmas-Hanukkah-Kwanza, you will need a vacation!*** No matter the celebration, the focus of students seems to be divided between two things: presents and candy. Let's start with the presents. First, the trauma that comes to students everywhere related to holiday presents cannot be overstated. Who is giving what to whom? Who isn't giving something to whom? Does a gift of a stuffed animal mean love? Are middle-school girls supposed to be shopping at Victoria's Secret®? Is it better to bring the presents on the last day before vacation or earlier? What is the social penalty for not giving a present to someone who gives you one? Does candy count as a present? Can said candy be consumed in class? And for the teachers, the question is usually the same: "When does vacation start?"

61 ***Presents for teachers are a big deal.*** Again, no one told me the importance this would take on. First, I am often surprised by the wonderful gifts students give me each year. Next, I am sometimes surprised by the hideous gifts I receive once in a while. Of course I'm grateful to be considered gift-worthy, but the plate of homemade-looking somethings with an unidentifiable smell will often give me pause, as will the notepads advertising someone's mom's business, or the two-foot candy cane, or the already opened "regifted" gift.

And don't kid yourself: teachers compare presents; we can be just as petty as any student out there!

62 ***Teachers run into difficulties when giving presents, too.*** The problem is that no one told me whether or not it was required to give gifts to all other teachers, all students, neither, both, or just the people I like. And don't forget the secretaries and custodians who, as I learned quickly, hold the real power in the school (see Chapter 10). Is a card too cheap? What about a card and a candy cane? How tacky is the plate of homemade somethings? Again I am usually left to ponder the one most important question: "When does vacation start!"

63 ***There will be more candy.*** The situation here is close to the one at Halloween, but red and white are substituted for orange and black. There will also be a faint peppermint smell everywhere for approximately two weeks before the holidays themselves. This holiday season also seems to bring out all forms of cookies. Fortunately most of these things culminate with time off for everyone to unwind from the trauma of gift giving and candy consumption. If you're like me, it will be at least three days into the December break before you can focus on the 'true meaning' of anything!

The next thing I was never taught relates to the first big holiday of the new year, and that is . . .

64 ***Valentine's Day brings unexpected stress to schools everywhere.*** Once again the focus seems to be candy, but this holiday has the added aspect of the one thing few students are capable of handling well: LOVE. Most elementary teachers deal with this issue by requiring every student to make or buy a Valentine for every other student. This limits the number of surprises but still causes some angst related to who gets what card. Another recent development is that a simple card is not enough for many overachieving families. The card-with-candy or even card-with-small-gift combination seems to be taking over classrooms everywhere. This will inevitably lead to teachers feeling that a gift of a simple valentine to each student is substandard. After just recovering from December, this will only increase the stress on teachers' creativity (and bank accounts).

In middle school when cards are usually not required, the stress caused by this holiday is unbearable for many early adolescents. Again, who gets a card? Who gets candy? What is the underlying message of giving or not giving? Many sleepless nights can be attributed to this mid-February ritual. I also personally enjoy seeing a love-struck eighth-grade boy carrying around a red stuffed bear (or dog or dragon or whatever) that he wouldn't have been caught dead with any other day of the year, but since it was a gift from the girl of his dreams . . . .

Next comes a holiday that began in one culture but has grown to have implications for Americans everywhere . . .

65 ***For many, St. Patrick's Day is just an excuse for people to pinch each other.*** Even though few of my students have actually been of Irish descent, the whole wear-green-or-get-pinched thing has permeated the school culture. Take my advice here and buy a packet of shamrock stickers, then give one to every student you see. The payoff for this small investment will be much less trauma regarding who's wearing what, what color people claim their undergarments are, etc. Fortunately for teachers everywhere, there is no St. Patrick's Day candy. Maybe it's coming . . . .

Each year as I begin to recover from March, I recall . . .

66 ***Something bad WILL happen on April Fools' Day.*** No one ever told me that the happiest teaching years I would have could often be directly correlated to years when April 1st fell on a weekend! Then there are the rest. April Fools' Day seems to say to students everywhere, "Whatever your boundaries are, break through them." Thus students who are predominantly without boundaries will find themselves pulling pranks like putting tacks on chairs, super-gluing locks, or pulling the fire alarm. The slightly more refined students may do things like rearrange furniture, hide under desks, or coordinate an effort to have everyone in the class drop their pencils at the same time.

I do have to admit, though, that my personal favorites are the clever but usually boundary-observing students. Some of their best efforts have included putting little plastic ants in my drawer, changing the computer desktop pictures to 80s album covers, and leaving a phone message pretending to be someone famous. In any case, I am always happy to see April 2nd arrive!

And speaking of holidays, whatever you do, . . .

67 ***Don't mess with Spring Break.*** Spring Break is as close to a national holiday as schools come without the legal proclamation. Somewhere in March or April, most schools participate in this time-honored tradition. While it isn't officially a legal holiday, try telling anyone in a school that Spring Break is cancelled and watch the mayhem unfold!

There are many things I wasn't told about Spring Break, including the fact that many students take much more exotic trips than I could ever imagine (or afford!). I always found it a bit annoying that the 14-year-olds came back from break looking tanned and rested.

Those who aren't willing or able to leave town can usually be found at your closest mall. If you need to do some shopping over Spring Break, be prepared to see many people you know! After all, it is during this time that spring fashions become important.

In my experience the actual weather outside has very little influence on what students (especially girls) are wearing. If the calendar says spring, the skimpy clothes begin to show up on students everywhere, and many of these are purchased over Spring Break!

After Spring Break, most students are counting down to summer, and the excitement over whatever holidays remain seems to wane. Luckily most teachers also have an extended summer break to relax and start preparing their Halloween costumes for next year!

Chapter 13

Interruptions

As a new teacher, I knew I would have to deal with everything related to the classroom. I was prepared for lesson planning, attendance, grading papers, classroom management, evaluations, and even a standardized test or two. But no one pointed out that . . .

68 ***There will be an astounding number of interruptions to your plans every single day.***

The list begins with . . .

69 ***Every school has "required" interruptions.*** These include daily announcements, monthly fire drills, and semiannual drills of different natures that will vary depending on the local climate and circumstances (we have tornado drills). These might also include scheduled interruptions like assemblies, visitors, or school construction. While I in no way diminish the importance of these activities, I had no idea the extent to which they would affect the actual teaching I'm able to accomplish.

Things get even more interesting when these required interruptions are augmented by other interruptions; for example, one year we had a fire drill on Halloween. Seeing all the little ghosts, witches, and princesses make their way through the slushy snow was very unsettling! Did I mention I was dressed up like a Dalmatian? I can only imagine what the school's neighbors thought. And the worst part of all was that this drill was only necessary because we were required to hold one every month, and no one had remembered to have the October drill until the 31st. It was completely preventable chaos!

The next category is the random interruption. I had no idea about the possibility that . . .

70 ***On any given day, your classes may be interrupted by secretaries, administrators, other teachers, other students, parents, repair workers, custodians, or anyone else within a three-block radius.*** Sometimes this means a drop-in visit, other times it's a phone call, and other times it's just an unexplained noise. When my building was new, it was not uncommon to see a district maintenance worker literally come down through the ceiling while working on a wiring issue. My school also has phones in each classroom, which can be a blessing but also a curse if a persistent textbook salesman gets a hold of your direct extension. This can also be a curse if you have angered the secretaries (see Chapter 10); all sorts of errant calls may come your way. Of course on some occasions these interruptions are necessary and relate to critical issues, but on many occasions they are not.

Next . . .

71 ***Do not expect to get anything accomplished in class if the weather outside is changing.*** That's right, weather is a major interruption. The first snowfall, the first warm spring day, the first thunderstorm, and anything unusual thereafter will cause a serious disturbance. You would think that kids who live here in Colorado have seen snow before, but whenever it falls during the school day the vast majority of them feel the need to say something to the effect of, "It's snowing!" and rush to the window if they think they can. And even when the comments are done and the kids are seated, an observant teacher can tell that very few minds are on the class work. This is also true for wind and rain.

The next category of interruption is fairly infrequent where I work, but its effects can be astounding: the humble "bug."

72 ***Any living creature in the classroom may as well be a man-eating shark for the interruption it causes.*** A tiny spider can cause a scream, a scream causes hysteria, and hysteria means nothing else is getting accomplished. This is of course magnified if it's a big spider or if the problem is exacerbated by a student who insists on catching it and dangling it in front of others. And spiders are nothing compared to the bee/hornet/wasp. While spiders are generally easy to get rid of, the bee/hornet/wasp is not. If your classroom has a high ceiling, this problem (and the accompanying hysteria) could go on for hours. Add to that the concern about bee sting allergies and you may as well give up your lesson and focus solely on the insect because everyone else will be.

Once in a while you may even get the rodent-on-the-loose interruption. This was prevalent right after my school was constructed, and even on the second floor we would sometimes see a tiny tail disappear under a door. In such instances, it is best to hope no one else notices and deal with it later (as in after class when no students are present).

This brings me to . . .

73 ***No matter the level of fear, it is you, the teacher, who is responsible for dispatching unwanted creatures as quickly and quietly as possible.*** This may mean taking off your shoe and squishing something or casually swatting something out of the air. If you are unwilling to do this, be prepared for the situation to escalate and all control to be lost. If the creature is large enough that you need to call for help (a bird, for example), write off the entire class period and probably the entire day because your class just became the talk of the school.

This next type of interruption may be somewhat unique to my school, but I doubt it. We have a group called the ERT, or Emergency Response Team. It is their job to be first on the scene if a student is suddenly ill or injured, and they do wonderful work. The problem is that in order to activate this team, someone in the office has to get on the intercom and make an announcement. When that happens, every student in the school is made aware that there is an emergency of some type somewhere. That is, . . .

74 ***One person's emergency rapidly becomes everyone's curiosity.*** Just like those who slow to watch a traffic accident, students feel the need to know who's been hurt and how badly. In my classroom I have a nice view of the playground, which happens to be the site of many an incident. Thus when the ERT is activated, there are always students who rush to the window and look out. It doesn't matter what is going on in class or how compelling I think it is, the window takes precedence. Fortunately these emergencies are usually short-lived, but in the event they aren't, it's possible to watch an entire class period disappear before your eyes.

The final type of interruption is much less serious in the long run, but not if you're thirteen. Just remember, . . .

75 ***School day wardrobe malfunctions are not to be taken lightly.*** A broken zipper, a ripped seam, torn straps, or ink stains all have the potential to be major interruptions for both genders. The wise teacher keeps safety pins and stain remover on hand at all times and takes care of any problems before they escalate.

If there is no easy way to repair something, get ready for the fact that . . .

76 ***Students can turn fixing a problem into much more of an ordeal than the actual problem.*** One example is the student who used an entire roll of masking tape to repair a hole in his shoe. Another would be the large number of my students who have tried to staple their clothes back together. And of course there are the students who feel the need to enlist all sorts of help, as in, "Can Jenny and Kelsey come to the bathroom with me to fix my shirt?" I do know that once a student decides they have a wardrobe malfunction, you would be better off to let them deal with it on the spot because they will be unable to accomplish anything else until they do.

The final category of interruptions is what I loosely refer to as "equipment problems." Amazingly, I have learned that . . .

77 ***Most anything in your classroom is capable of malfunctioning and derailing your plan for the day.*** Things I have personally experienced that fall into this category include a podium coming apart, overhead projector bulb burn-outs, dead remote control batteries, a jammed stapler, a power outage, blinking fluorescent light bulbs, and a bent table leg. These don't include the malfunctions that are student-caused like spills, broken chairs, or (my personal favorite) ink messes. I had no idea that pens could "explode," but if I had a dollar for every student who told me that was the cause of his ink-stained hands/face/paper, I would be retiring early!

Chapter 14

Bodily Functions

First, a disclaimer: this chapter is not for the squeamish! While I will do my best to use euphemisms when possible, if you are not up to reading about bodily functions, school, and the sometimes unseemly combination of the two, move ahead to chapter 15!

That said, no one ever told me that . . .

78 ***Bodily functions will play an important role in the classroom!*** I come from a family of people who really don't discuss their bodily functions, and I like it that way. Imagine my horror the first time two boys decided to have a "fart contest" in the middle of my class, or the sweet-looking girl who demonstrated her ability to burp out the entire alphabet. Then there was the time a boy raised his hand, asked to use the restroom, and proceeded to give graphic details of exactly what he was planning to do in there. Aargh! That doesn't even count the bodily malfunctions like bloody noses and throwing up. One of my most horrifying experiences may or may not technically qualify as a bodily function, but it's bodily-related: I once had a student ask to go to his locker, and while he was gone he proceeded to pierce his own eyebrow. Turns out he had borrowed a friend's earring to do the deed after being dared by an attractive classmate. Apparently he didn't think I'd notice, but it was hard to miss. When he returned, he was covering his eyebrow with his hand and was obviously in some pain. No one ever told me that one of my very own students might impale himself on purpose. (In case you're wondering, he was immediately sent to the nurse's office, then sent home, then taken to the doctor's office for repairs. He returned with a stitch and a huge bandage, neither of which impressed the girl he was interested in!)

The good news is that I also learned very quickly that . . .

79 ***Good teachers learn to fake being nonchalant.*** The more I react with horror to such pronouncements of vulgarity, the bigger the reaction of the rest of the class. The better response is normally something unusual, such as, "I think you need more fiber in your diet," or "Do you need to go see the nurse?" I have also helped myself by placing the tissue box far from my desk, so perpetual nose blowers can keep their distance. The little things can make all the difference!

Another aspect of this topic is the fact that students will ask your permission to attend to their needs. Nobody ever told me . . .

80 ***I have the power to "let them go" or not!*** Seriously, what other job in the world has people asking for your approval to use the restroom? It's a little surreal when you think about it.

And then . . .

81 ***There will be "accidents."*** Of course the frequency, type, and severity vary by age, but I don't know any teacher who has been in the classroom more than five years who has not been affected by a classroom accident of one sort or another. In such cases, I recommend quick action (usually involving the custodian) and a revisit of Number 79. In worst cases, a classroom evacuation may be necessary, so have a plan.

And in case you think accidents are limited to students, I will recount an incident from not too many years ago. It seems that the boy with muscular dystrophy hadn't noticed his service dog eating staples from the carpet. When those staples hit "Buster's" digestive system, he purged them, along with all his lunch, onto the classroom carpet (and made some rather nasty coughing sounds as well). This accident was made even more memorable by the autistic boy who felt the need to describe the stain and its contents for the rest of the class. Honestly all I could do was laugh, call the custodian, and be thankful that there was another adult in the room with me to witness the mayhem. Who could have guessed!

Next is . . .

82 ***Spit is important to students.*** This usually takes the form of chewing on something that shouldn't be chewed on, but it may also take the form of drooling or the dreaded spit wad. One time after disciplining a student for spitting a wad of paper across the room, I was informed (by the student of course) that he wasn't actually spitting—he was "throwing with his mouth." He seemed to be able to blend bodily functions with excuse making in a rather unique way!

In a related issue, I had no idea that . . .

83 ***During the day, teachers generally aren't allowed to have bodily functions.*** I guess I should have known this from my own school days, because I don't ever remember seeing a teacher go to the restroom in 12 years. I think people were even more private then, too, and the faculty restroom was probably hidden in a cave somewhere deep in the building. At any rate, I had no idea that once I began teaching I would have to stifle all my personal needs during the school day.

Not only is there no time to use the restroom, but there are plenty of reasons to avoid doing so altogether. First, teachers risk letting on that they are human; many students would be deeply distressed to discover that teachers need a restroom at all.

Second, going to the restroom means that much time when you're not paying attention to your surroundings, and the possibilities for problems multiply exponentially when that happens.

Third, there are the innate risks of restroom use: unzipped flies, toilet paper on shoes, skirts inadvertently tucked into tights, unexplained splash stains, etc.

And finally, there is a risk at my school that comes courtesy of the latest technology: the self-flush toilets and automatic faucets. Here are two specific examples of problems these have caused:

> First, I once placed all of my school mail on top of the sink while I used the toilet. Gravity caused the mail to fall into the sink, and that triggered the automatic faucet to turn on. My mail became a saturated mess while I sat and watched.
>
> Second, it is a common occurrence at my school for a teacher to accidentally flush something down the toilet. It works like this: the teacher sits down, the cell phone/ID badge/bracelet falls into the water, and when the teacher stands up to grab for it, the toilet flushes. Down it goes, followed by a call to the city's sanitation department. The "lucky" ones recover their items, although seldom in working condition!

In worst cases, when you absolutely have to succumb to the urge to answer nature's call during the school day, remember . . .

84 ***Never try to use the restroom when you're in a hurry.*** Rather, use due caution and allow plenty of time to take care of any unforeseen issues that may arise, because they probably will.

Chapter 15

Unexpected Responsibilities

All teachers know that the job is full of responsibilities. These include supervision, planning, instruction, establishing a sense of community and rapport, following district and state guidelines, and being a generally good citizen. What I didn't know was . . .

85 ***Teachers have dozens of miscellaneous responsibilities that no one warned me about.*** Some of these are required responsibilities and some of them are just suggested, but taking them all seriously will, in most cases, make teachers better.

The first category includes . . .

86 ***Be prepared for many unexpected responsibilities during the school day.*** You need to know that there are all sorts of things to do in addition to your actual job description, and you will need to accomplish them in your "spare" time. Some of these relate directly to students, but some do not. These include everything from the mundane, such as supervising lunches or hallways, to the horrible, such as calling the Department of Social Services about cases of abuse or neglect. Somewhere in between these extremes would be things like "Spirit Days" when everyone dresses up according to a theme, covering classes for colleagues in an emergency, or answering someone else's phone extension to make it stop ringing.

Another odd responsibility I experience regularly is taste testing all sorts of interesting food prepared by the cooking class. I can only begin to describe the macaroni and cheese that looked like modeling clay, the rice pudding that looked like glue, or the curried mystery casserole that didn't look like anything recognizable at all. Yet I tried them, and so did my teammates, not because we were hungry but because the 'chefs' were proud and wanted to share. And once in a while this responsibility has the positive outcome of a tasty mid-day snack!

The next thing to know is that . . .

87 ***The school day is never actually confined to the school day.*** In other words, there will be dances after school, supervision before school, meetings at all hours, grading at home, committee functions, parent nights, sporting events, and club meetings. The extent of these responsibilities will vary, but they exist in every school I've ever known. In addition, there will be events you are not required to go to but will feel the need to attend anyway because your students are so eager to show off. You might find yourself at a karate graduation, a piano recital, a cheerleading competition, or a religious rite of passage. All of these can be a pleasant but unexpected part of the job.

A less pleasant aspect is . . .

88 ***Teachers have homework, too.*** Although there are many strategies to ease your take-home work load, there will be times when you will find yourself grading, writing, scheduling, and preparing at home. How much and how often depend on what you're teaching, how comfortable you are with your lessons, and how many times you were interrupted during the school day when you were trying to get these things done (see Chapter 13). During my first year of teaching, I spent two to three hours at home every day just trying to figure out what I was going to do the next day. That situation has gotten better, but now as an English teacher I find I cannot do students' work (especially their writing) justice unless I take it home and spend some quality time with it. This doesn't even take into account the amount of reading required to keep up with available young adult literature, not to mention keeping up with educational research and trends.

And finally, there is the responsibility of staying current with popular culture. This means . . .

89 ***Good teachers watch a bunch of junk on television that they normally wouldn't go near under any circumstances.*** The exact shows and network will vary based on your preferences; for me it usually involves watching skateboarding pranksters or scantily clad coeds living together and being filmed in all sorts of compromising positions. Yet if these shows are influencing the students, they're indirectly influencing the teacher, and that means it's a good idea to watch sometimes even if you feel it is causing premature demise of your brain cells. The same is true for music, magazines, games, and web sites. If you feel your self-respect declining by the minute, just tell yourself it's research. Remember, if you fall too far behind the popular references of your students, you will lose their respect, and we all know where that's heading (see Chapter 1!).

Chapter 16

Other Strange Surprises

After a short time on the job, I learned . . .

90 ***Teachers say the strangest things!*** I had no idea that phrases like "spit out your gum" or "pull up your pants" would come out of my mouth on a regular basis. In fact, these have become such a prevalent part of my vocabulary that it is not uncommon for me to give these instructions to strangers at the mall. I also never expected to say random things such as "Why are you writing on yourself?" "Stop tipping your chair," or "Don't eat your pencil." Every now and then I pause and reflect on these strange pronouncements, at which time I find it's usually better not to!

My next surprise was . . .

91 ***Society makes lots of assumptions about teachers.*** These include things like all teachers are Democrats, all teachers belong to a union, all teachers are married, all teachers want to be administrators when they grow up, all teachers are clueless about fashion, and all middle-school teachers secretly wish they were teaching high school. Specific subject-related assumptions include all P.E. teachers are frustrated college athletes, all English teachers are frustrated writers, all drama teachers are frustrated actors, and all band directors are frustrated musicians. Some of this probably stems from the old adage, "Those who can't do, teach." I would say that anyone who still believes these assumptions needs to spend more time in their local school talking to the teachers!

Next, I was surprised to learn . . .

92 ***Most students are genuinely shocked to see teachers outside of the classroom.*** As mentioned in Chapter 14, I never saw any of my own teachers use the restroom. I can add that I never saw them shopping, getting haircuts, going out to dinner, or experiencing any of the normal things I'm sure they did when I wasn't looking. It follows, then, that I shouldn't be surprised to hear students shrieking my name when they see me at the mall, or asking what I'm doing at the grocery store. But I am surprised! Even in today's world there is still a bit of a mystique about what teachers are up to when they're not teaching, and students who encounter you outside of school can react in all sorts of strange ways. They may, as previously mentioned, shriek with delight. They may also run and hide, ask what you're buying, or feel the need to introduce you to everyone they're with. In any case, it's unlikely they will just say "hi" and keep walking, so expect some interesting encounters!

The next thing I was never directly taught has proven helpful in all sorts of situations. That is . . .

93 ***Few skills are as important to a teacher as self-restraint.*** Over the course of your career, you WILL want to do some or all of the following: yell at students, curse in class, roll your eyes, insult others, make faces, tell secrets, smack someone, throw an object across the room, or say something untoward you're *really* thinking at any given moment. Don't do it. Find yourself a trustworthy friend or a loyal dog and share your inner frustrations with them. You will thank yourself later!

"It makes no sense to worry about the future. By the time you get there, it's the past!"

Chapter 17

A Few Final Amazing and Happy Things

By nature, teachers often have to generalize their instruction in order to reach the greatest number of students in a limited amount of time and space; it follows that much of your time will be spent with groups, both large and small. Additionally, most teachers assume that their students will be a lot like they were back in school. Some will, but many won't. In any case, don't ever overlook that . . .

94 ***Some of the best surprises come from getting to know one student at a time.*** It isn't easy to find the time to do this, but it is worth it. Thus the last few things no one prepared me for in education school relate to individual students and the unique things you will learn from them if you are willing to listen.

95 ***Students will surprise you with their neediness.*** There are so many kids out there who just need to be heard. They may feel like no one listens to them, or they may feel misunderstood or lonely. They may have unfortunate home lives, or they may just want the opinion of someone they respect. This is especially true for adolescents who are, even under the best circumstances, dealing with major changes in just about every aspect of their lives. As a teacher, you are in a unique position to influence their choices, and this is not a responsibility that should ever be taken lightly.

96 ***Students will surprise you with their willingness to open up.*** When you do listen, you will be amazed at what students have to say. Right there in your school are artistic geniuses, philosophers, musicians, travelers, fashion experts, and athletes. There are also kids who are dying to tell you about their accomplishments, their fears, and their goals for the future.

Occasionally this unabashed openness can lead to the disclosure of sensitive information; for example you may learn about a student's dying relative, someone with an eating disorder, or a drug problem. In such cases you will need to consult an administrator or counselor to see what types of follow-up are necessary. These disclosures will sometimes rip at your heart, but in my experience that always beats the alternative of deciding not to care.

97 ***Students will surprise you with their resilience.*** I have been astounded over the years to see students who have faced monumental challenges and come out happy and healthy on the other side. Whether it's a personal issue, an academic issue, a family issue, or any combination of those, most students learn to adjust and move forward. If you can play any part in this transformation, consider yourself fortunate.

Here are just a couple of the hundreds of examples of resilience I have witnessed. First is a seventh-grade boy whose older sister committed suicide during the school year. He stopped doing his work, grew his hair out to cover his eyes, hardly spoke, and seemed to have no desire even to finish middle school. His other teachers and I weren't even sure he'd survive, not to mention thrive. Eight years later I saw him at a local sporting event; he had become a handsome and confident young man, and I hardly recognized him. He remembered me, introduced himself, and said he had graduated from college and was now working as an English teacher in a poor village in Mexico. He showed me pictures of his young students and spoke about how proud he was of doing work he loved.

My next example is an eighth-grade girl who hadn't done much of anything academic since she turned twelve. Despite counseling, tutoring, summer school, and frustrated parents and teachers, she had failing grades in every subject. Some time in the middle of eighth grade, she decided it was time to prepare herself for high school. Just like that, she started working hard, asking for help, and caring about her future, and she turned her entire world around. When I followed up two years later, she was on the honor roll at our local high school. Hoping I could take advantage of whatever strategy she had employed, I asked her what happened. Unfortunately for the other nonperforming students, she had no explanation other than "something just clicked." While I certainly wouldn't recommend this route to academic success, it does give hope to the students out there who seem to be unreachable. Often they are being reached; it's just taking time for them to realize it!

Beyond those two specific stories are the kids who survive learning disabilities, accidents, illnesses, divorce, the loss of a parent, unplanned pregnancies, relocation, and infinite other issues. You will also find many students who 'survive' issues that you may not find serious but they certainly do, like fights with friends, embarrassing moments, or a failed test. Through it all, if you take the time to notice their strength, you will often find yourself stronger, too.

98 ***Students will surprise you with their knowledge.*** When I first started teaching, I felt it was critical to know everything. This included all there was to know about every lesson, every book, every author, and every grammar rule. After all, I reasoned, isn't that what teachers are for? It turns out that another thing I didn't know is that it is impossible to know everything! Very quickly I discovered there would always be things I didn't know, and even more surprising was the fact that there were often students who could fill me in.

My advice on this front is two-fold. First, let go of trying to know everything and just admit you don't (see Number 16). Second, after admitting you don't know something, ask your students. I guarantee this will make you a happier person and a better teacher, plus it opens up all sorts of possibilities for actually learning new things and modeling the learning process.

For example, the first time I taught the works of Edgar Allan Poe, the students immediately noticed from his brief biography in the textbook that he died at a fairly young age. The inevitable question was, "What did he die from?" After briefly considering making something up, I instead admitted the truth: I had no idea. I asked the class if they had heard anything, and several of them thought they remembered something about a disease, a heart attack, or a murder. No one could say for sure, though, and this led to a wonderful discussion of the possibilities of the time period, followed by a list of places we could look to find the answer. The next day, several students and I reported back to the class and compared our notes, and the feeling that we were all learning something new was powerful to everyone.

99 ***Students will surprise you with their abilities (if you let them).*** While it is possible to unearth students' hidden talents during routine classroom activities, my most astounding results have come when I have assigned more open-ended projects and watched what happened. In my first year of teaching Greek Mythology, for example, I assigned small groups to choose an original Olympian, conduct some research, and present their information to the class. (I should disclose that this was mostly out of self-preservation since I hadn't been in a mythology class myself since the eighth grade and was struggling to stay one chapter ahead.)

What followed was a group of students who produced an amazing video about the 12 labors of Hercules. Their special effects included transforming Mom's Buick into a giant Cretan bull (with horns) so they could "capture" it, constructing miniature Augean stables in a sandbox so they could "flood" them, and dressing their dogs up like the cattle of Geryon. They added music, title sequences, and even outtakes. It was unforgettable.

Another fabulous product came from a young lady who decided to demonstrate her knowledge of Colonial America by designing, writing, illustrating, and editing a magazine she called Colonial Teen. She included articles like "How to Lose Weight while Churning Butter," "Sew your own Bonnet in Five Easy Steps," and "The Boston Tea Party's Hottest Bachelors." To me this was the perfect convergence of what she knew and what she had researched, and I never would have seen any of it if I hadn't been willing to let go of some structure and see what she could do.

Of course there will be struggling students who barely do the required amount, but I have found that when I am prepared to learn as much from the students as I am prepared to teach them, the surprises never stop.

Next to last, but hardly least, there is . . .

100 ***Students will surprise you with their generosity and compassion.*** Sometimes the acts of kindness will be small, such as offering a vacant seat to a new student or loaning out a pencil (without throwing it!). Other times the generosity and compassion will happen on a large scale, and I have found this to be especially true when someone is in genuine need. Kids really do want to make a difference in the world, and sometimes all they are waiting for is the opportunity.

To illustrate this, I only have to go back to the beginning of the 2007–2008 school year when one of our own teachers was diagnosed with lung cancer. He was just 58 years old and appeared extremely healthy, so we were all shocked to learn that his prognosis was dire. When the news was passed on to the students, the shows of compassion began. At first there were cards, posters, and good wishes. As things got worse and his expenses skyrocketed, the fundraising began. Parents and teachers worked hard and raised money, but the most touching efforts came from the students. Among other things, every Friday became "Hat Day for Mr. Romero." The kids were allowed to wear hats in our usually no-hats-allowed school with a suggested donation of $1 or more. In truth the hats were just to remind us of the cause, and it was inspirational to see so many participate. The results were amazing; kids were wearing all sorts of hats to support their teacher, and along with that came hundreds of dollars each week. One student had a huge bottle of quarters that he decided to donate; even after he found out it totaled more than $1100, he wanted to give it all away.

Mr. Romero died on the Fourth of July, 2008. He was an inspiration to everyone he knew, and especially the students who will never forget all the things he taught them. For our entire community he also provided the opportunity for us to be better people by showing we cared. He left this world knowing that he was loved and realizing that his influence reached far beyond what he had previously known.

• • •

I used to think teaching was all about the students. I now know that while students are the center of teaching, there is much more. The job called "teaching" in fact includes talking, listening, learning, reflecting, avoiding, reacting, responding, sharing, caring, reading, writing, planning, meeting, and occasionally panicking. Through it all I have found that the best surprise has been . . .

101 ***If your attitude is right and you expect the unexpected, teaching will be the toughest AND best job you will ever have.***